Snow White
and the
Seven Dwarfs

Retold by Lesley Sims

Illustrated by
Desideria Guicciardini

Reading consultant: Alison Kelly
Roehampton University

Contents

Chapter 1

As white as snow

One winter's day, a young
Queen stood sewing by her
window. As she watched the
feathery snowflakes fall, her
needle slipped.

Three drops of ruby-red blood fell onto the snow. The Queen sighed. "I wish I had a child," she said, "with skin as white as snow, lips as red as blood and hair as black as ebony wood."

Her wish came true.

The Queen's daughter had skin as white as snow, lips as red as blood and hair as black as ebony.

The King was delighted and named her Snow White. But his joy was mixed with misery, for the young Queen died.

"My child needs a mother," he thought. Within a year, he had married again.

His new wife was proud and vain. Her heart was so full of love for herself, she had none for anyone else.

The only thing she wanted was to be the most beautiful woman in the world.

Morning and night, she
gazed into her magic mirror
and asked the same question.

Mirror, mirror on the
wall, who's the fairest
of us all?

And, morning
and night, the
mirror replied,
"You are."

The new Queen paid no attention to Snow White, who grew more lovely every day.

Then, one dreadful morning, the Queen asked, "Mirror, mirror on the wall, who's the fairest of us all?" and the mirror said...

Actually, it's Snow White!

The Queen went pink with
rage and her beautiful face
scowled into the mirror. "I
won't have it,"
she snarled.

Whenever the Queen asked
her question, the mirror gave
the same reply. Finally, she
could bear it no longer. "Snow
White must die!" she decided.

Chapter 2

A deadly plan

The Queen called for the royal huntsman, her heart bursting with jealousy.

"Take Snow White to the forest and kill her," she ordered. "I can't stand her near me."

The huntsman was horrified, but he had to obey.

Snow White chatted happily
as they went into the forest.
The huntsman didn't say a
word. Under a giant oak tree,
he took out a knife and pulled
her from her horse.

"What are you doing?" she
shouted in alarm.

12

"Queen's orders," said the huntsman, sadly. "She wants me to... kill you."

"What?" cried Snow White. "No! Please, let me go," she begged. Her dark eyes filled with tears and the huntsman took pity on her.

As he stood there, he spotted a wild pig in the distance. "I'll take its lungs and liver to the Queen," he thought, "and Snow White will be safe."

He turned to Snow White. "Run, then," he said, "but never return to the palace."

Chapter 3

Deep in the forest

Snow White ran,
past twisty trees
and scratchy
brambles. Soon,
her black hair
was tangled
with leaves.

She ran until the sun sank
and the forest grew dark.
Thorny branches like witches'
fingers reached out to catch
her. Still she ran. She ran until
her legs could barely
hold her...

...and then she saw a cottage.
"Maybe someone here can
help me," she thought.

16

To her dismay, there was no one home. She leaned against the door to catch her breath and it swung open. Snow White stumbled inside.

The first thing she saw was a tiny table and seven tiny chairs. Snow White smelled fresh bread and honey and her mouth watered.

17

After running all day, she
was starving. Sitting down,
she helped herself to bread and
honey and drank every drop
of milk from all seven mugs.

18

She put down the last mug
and yawned. Running all day
was exhausting.

Seven tiny beds with fat
pillows stood along one wall.

Snow White
tried bed after bed.
The first was too hard, the
second too narrow... By the
seventh, she was so tired, she
curled up on it anyway.

While Snow White slept, the cottage door opened and seven dwarfs trooped in. They each lit a candle and looked around in surprise.

20

Quietly, they gathered
around Snow White and
watched her sleeping.

Her hair's as
black as ebony.

Her skin's as
white as snow.

Her lips are
as red as blood.

"She's beautiful,"
they all sighed together.

Next morning, Snow White
was woken by seven songs
sung very badly. She jumped
out of bed in a panic – but the
dwarfs were so friendly, she
forgot to be afraid.

When she told them about
the Queen, the dwarfs were
disgusted. "Stay here," they
said. "We'll take care of you."

Chapter 4

Pretty silks to sell

In her palace bedroom, the Queen was singing too. Smiling at her reflection, she asked her usual question.

Mirror, mirror on the wall, who's the fairest of us all?

"Well Queen, you are fair, no doubt about it," the mirror said chattily. "But Snow White is fairer. She's living in a cottage in the forest," it added.

"Snow White is alive?" the Queen spat in fury. "That huntsman tricked me!"

She was so angry she couldn't eat or sleep. Instead, she spent every second plotting how to kill Snow White.

At last, she disguised herself as an old pedlar. Packing a basket with ribbons and silks, she set off for the forest.

Snow White was cleaning the cottage when an old woman came to the door.

"Pretty things to sell," the woman cackled. "Silks and satins, belts and bows."

"What lovely silks," cried Snow White, stroking a belt.

"Here, my dear," said the old woman. "Try it on."

She looped the belt around Snow White's waist and pulled it tight... tighter and tighter...

The woman kept pulling until Snow White collapsed.

The dwarfs came home to find Snow White lying in the doorway. Shocked, they saw the belt squeezing the life out of her.

Whipping out a knife, one of the dwarfs sliced through it. Snow White spluttered and began to breathe again.

"Where's the old pedlar woman?" she gasped.

"What old woman?" a dwarf began. "No one knows we're here..." He gave a sudden shout. "Hey! It must have been that wicked Queen. She tricked you."

The dwarfs looked serious.

"You're in grave danger,"
said one.

"The Queen will keep trying
to kill you," said another.

"Don't open the door!" they
all said together.

Meanwhile, the wicked Queen had run all the way home and raced to her mirror.

Mirror, mirror on the wall, who's the fairest of us all?

Sit down your majesty.

It's still Snow White.

The next day, the Queen
was back at the cottage with
a poisoned comb. But Snow
White refused to let her in.

"You can look, can't you?"
said the Queen, holding the
sparkly comb to the window.

Snow White
was entranced.
Forgetting her
promise, she
opened the door.

Quicker than a bee, the Queen darted inside and stuck the comb in Snow White's hair. The poison worked at once and she fell to the floor.

As soon as the dwarfs saw Snow White, they knew the Queen had returned.

"Look what she's done now!" said one, taking out the comb.

Snow White moaned. "Oh, my head..."

"You must be more careful," the dwarfs warned her. "The Queen will try again. DON'T open the door!"

Chapter 5

The magic apple

Before you ask, it's still Snow White.

At the palace, the Queen's heart was eaten up with envy. She hated being the second fairest. Angrily, she set to work on her worst spell yet.

In a secret room, the Queen made a magic apple. It looked so delicious, whoever saw it would have to eat it. But she dipped one half in poison.

Then she dressed up as a farmer's wife and went to the cottage once more.

"I won't buy anything,"
Snow White called out to her,
"and I mustn't open the door."

"I'm not selling," said the
Queen quickly. "I just thought
you'd like to share this apple."

She held out a shiny red apple. "Mmm, very juicy," she added. She took a large bite out of one side and licked her lips. "Here, try it."

"It does look good," agreed Snow White, and took a bite too. That instant, she fell to the ground in a crumpled heap.

39

The Queen laughed. "White as snow, red as blood, black as wood – and dead as dead! At last I'm the most beautiful woman in the world!"

Chapter 6

A prince rides by

"Not again!" groaned a dwarf, when he saw Snow White sprawled on the floor. But this time, they couldn't help her.

No belt.

No comb. She's dead...

"She's so beautiful," sobbed the youngest dwarf. "We can't bury her." So they laid her in a glass coffin and wrote *The Princess Snow White* upon it. They placed the coffin on a nearby hill and took turns keeping watch.

Snow White had been there
for over a year when a prince
rode by. He saw her skin as
white as snow, her lips as red
as blood and her hair as black
as ebony, and he fell in love.

Leaping from his horse, he knelt by the coffin. "She's beautiful," he said to the dwarf guarding her.

Please let me take her to my palace.

What? No!

"I want to build a splendid tomb for her," said the prince. "A princess belongs in a palace."

The dwarfs argued with the prince all day, but by sunset, they agreed. Almost at once, he was back with servants to carry the coffin.

As they lifted it, one tripped. The coffin slipped and the apple flew from Snow White's mouth. To their astonishment, she opened her eyes.

The prince was overjoyed.
He flung open the coffin,
swept her up and carried her
to his horse.

Meanwhile, the Queen was
going back to her mirror.

"Snow White is fairest. Ask me another," said the mirror saucily before she could speak.

With a furious cry, the Queen smashed her mirror into a thousand pieces. And a thousand glass splinters chorused, "Snow White is still the fairest of them all."

The story of *Snow White and the Seven Dwarfs* has been around since the thirteenth century and was told by storytellers all over Europe. This version is based on the retelling by Jacob and Wilhelm Grimm, two brothers who lived in Germany in the early 1800s.

Designed by Natacha Goransky
Cover design by Russell Punter

First published in 2005 by Usborne Publishing Ltd., Usborne House, 83-85 Saffron Hill, London EC1N 8RT, England. www.usborne.com
Copyright © 2005 Usborne Publishing Ltd.

48